CONTENTS

RACERS

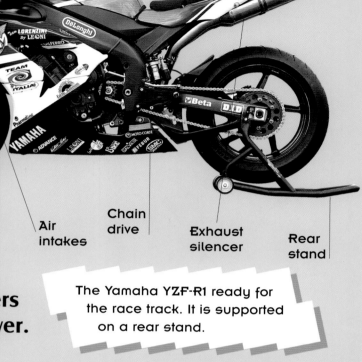

Air intakes

Chain drive

Exhaust silencer

Rear stand

Big engines, terrifying top speeds and high-tech materials; these are the features of the world's biggest racing motorcycles, the superbikes. These machines compete in the World Superbike (WSB) championship. Only expert riders can control their awesome power.

The Yamaha YZF-R1 ready for the race track. It is supported on a rear stand.

TEAM RACER

The Yamaha YZF-R1 is the superbike raced by the riders of the official Yamaha WSB team. With its combination of a light-weight aluminium frame and a powerful engine, it has all the ingredients of a top performer.

FORCED AIR

The Yamaha's engine has a 'forced air induction' system for more power. When the bike is moving forwards, air is pushed into ducts in the front fairing, forcing air into the engine's cylinders. This allows more fuel to be burned – giving extra power!

YAMAHA YZF-R1

TYPE	Track superbike
WEIGHT	162 kg (360 lb)
ENGINE CAPACITY	998 cc
ENGINE LAYOUT	In-line four
POWER	180 hp
TOP SPEED	310 kph (193 mph)

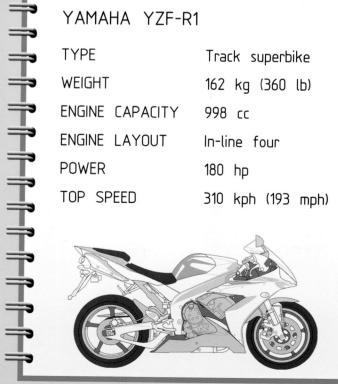

HONDA HORSEPOWER

The Honda CBR1000RR Fireblade is the most powerful racing superbike of all. Its four-cylinder engine has a power output of more than 200 horsepower (hp) (that's three times the power of a family-car engine). In top gear it reaches 300 kilometres/hour (186 miles/hour). That's a staggering 83 metres (272 feet) per second! The bike drives in a straight line using an electronically controlled steering damper, which stops the front wheel wobbling from side to side.

The Honda CBR1000RR superbike is raced by several of the teams in the World Superbike championship.

HONDA CBR1000RR FIREBLADE

TYPE	Track superbike
WEIGHT	165 kg (364 lb)
ENGINE CAPACITY	998 cc
ENGINE LAYOUT	In-line four
POWER	200 hp-plus
TOP SPEED	300 kph (186 mph)

web

FINDER

www.yamaha-racing.com
Site of the official Yamaha WSB team.
www.superbike.it
The Superbike World championship official site.

998-cc engine

Front disc brakes

STREET SUPERBIKES

Superbikes are not just for racing on the track. Most are also manufactured in road-going versions. These have all the extras, such as mirrors and registration plates, needed to make them 'street legal', as well as state-of-the-art technology borrowed from track racers.

Six-speed gearbox

Polymer fairing

The Ducati 999 Testastretta is based on a lightweight frame made up of steel tubes welded together.

DUCATI 999 TESTASTRETTA

TYPE	Road-going superbike
WEIGHT	186 kg (410 lb)
ENGINE CAPACITY	998 cc
ENGINE LAYOUT	L-twin
POWER	124 hp
TOP SPEED	270 kph (168 mph)

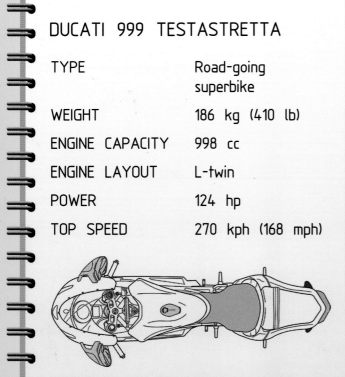

DREAM DUCATI

Ducati is the Ferrari of the motorcycle world. The stunning Ducati 999 Testastretta is Ducati's most high-performance and technically advanced bike. It's the dream bike of most motorcycle enthusiasts. The twin-cylinder Testastretta engine was developed for the track, and pushes the bike to a top speed of 270 kilometres/hour (168 miles/hour).

The BMW K1200S is one of the few superbikes to feature a front suspension arm instead of straight suspension forks.

SHAFT DRIVE BIKE

The BMW K1200S is the most powerful superbike that BMW has ever built. It borrows engine technology from BMW's Formula 1 car engines. The engine can accelerate the bike from a standstill to 100 kilometres/hour (62 miles/hour) in just 2.8 seconds. A unique feature of the K1200S is the lightweight shaft drive that carries power from the engine to the rear wheel. Other superbikes have a chain drive, which is a heavier system.

BMW
K1200S

TYPE	Road-going superbike
WEIGHT	248 kg (547 lb)
ENGINE CAPACITY	1,157 cc
ENGINE LAYOUT	In-line four
POWER	167 hp
TOP SPEED	200 kph (124 mph)

Indicators in mirrors

Front suspension arm

Alloy wheels

web

FINDER
www.ducati.com
Official Ducati website.
www.bmw.com
Official BMW website.

ON TOUR

Touring bikes are the giants of the motorcycle world. They are built for comfort on long-distance journeys. But that doesn't make them slow! Tourers have a passenger seat, luggage space and lots of gadgets.

KING OF THE ROAD

The Honda Gold Wing is the most famous touring bike in the world. The first Gold Wing was made in 1975. Its monstrous six-cylinder, 1,832-cc engine is more powerful than most car engines. The Gold Wing features advanced gadgets such as an electric motor for reversing, cruise control, computer-controlled suspension, and ABS brakes for safe braking in the wet.

The Honda Gold Wing is an impressive 2.64 m (8.66 ft) long. Its six-cylinder engine drives the rear wheel using a shaft.

HONDA GOLD WING

TYPE	Big tourer
WEIGHT	363 kg (800 lb)
ENGINE CAPACITY	1,832 cc
ENGINE LAYOUT	Horizontally opposed six
POWER	117 hp
TOP SPEED	190 kph (118 mph)

Radio aerial

Panniers

Passenger seat

Driver seat

Six-cylinder engine

Front forks

Exhaust
pipe

Panniers

Passenger
seat

V-twin
engine

The Harley-Davidson Road Glide
is a giant touring machine from
the famous American manufacturer.

STREET GLIDER

The Harley-Davidson FLTRI Road Glide is the
latest big touring bike from the famous
American manufacturer. Like all of Harley-
Davidson's big bikes, it is powered by a 1,450 cc,
V-twin engine. That means it has two giant
cylinders arranged in a V shape. The engine
makes a throaty, throbbing roar that sounds
like no other engine! It is only drowned out
by the bike's 40-watt stereo, hi-fi speakers.

FINDER

www.honda.co.uk/motorcycles
Official site of Honda motorcycles.
www.harley-davidson.com
Official site of Harley-Davidson motorcycles.

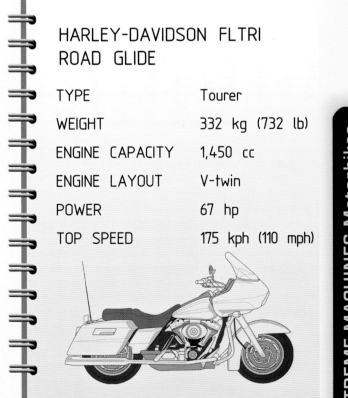

HARLEY-DAVIDSON FLTRI
ROAD GLIDE

TYPE	Tourer
WEIGHT	332 kg (732 lb)
ENGINE CAPACITY	1,450 cc
ENGINE LAYOUT	V-twin
POWER	67 hp
TOP SPEED	175 kph (110 mph)

DIRT BIKES

Protective
skid plate

Suspension
springs

Motorcycles designed for travelling across the countryside feature super-strong suspensions to cope with bumpy ground and chunky tyres to grip the mud. They are used for cross-country racing and for transport on farms.

The Honda CRF 450R powers into the air in a freestyle jumping competition.

MOTOCROSS MOTOR

The Honda CRF 450R is possibly the best dirt bike in the world. The powerful 450-cc engine drives it effortlessly through dirt and mud, and it is a popular choice for motocross riders, trials riders, stunt riders and rally riders. The front suspension springs and rear shock absorber squash down ('travel' is the technical word) by over 30 centimetres (12 inches) to absorb bone-crunching landings after jumps.

HONDA CRF 450R	
TYPE	Dirt bike
WEIGHT	99 kg (218 lb)
ENGINE CAPACITY	450 cc
ENGINE LAYOUT	Single
POWER	55 hp
TOP SPEED	130 kph (81 mph)

FOUR-WHEEL RACER

A quad bike is a motorcycle with four wheels instead of the usual two. Quad bikes feature motorcycle-style engines, frames and suspensions. The Bombardier DS650 Baja is a sports quad, and the fastest quad bike around, with a top speed of 120 kilometres/hour (75 miles/hour). The DS650 was also the only quad bike to complete the gruelling 11,000-kilometre (6,835-mile) Dakar Rally in 2004.

Motorcycle-style controls on handlebars

Skid plate

BOMBARDIER DS650 BAJA

TYPE	Sports quad bike
WEIGHT	213 kg (470 lb)
ENGINE CAPACITY	653 cc
ENGINE LAYOUT	Single
POWER	39 hp
TOP SPEED	120 kph (75 mph)

web

FINDER
www.honda.co.uk/motorcycles
Official site of Honda motorcycles.
www.bombardier-atv.com/enUS/Vehicles/2005/DS650
Details of the Bombardier quad bike.

The Bombardier DS650 features independent suspension on each wheel.

SIDECARS

The Hannigan GTL features electronic controls to keep the bike upright.

Glass-reinforced plastic body shell

Honda Gold Wing

Footplate

A sidecar is a small passenger compartment attached to the side of a motorcycle. Sidecars are normally bolted on to touring bikes, but there are racing sidecars too. A motorcycle and sidecar combination cannot lean over as a motorcycle on its own can.

HANNIGAN GTL

TYPE	Touring sidecar
WEIGHT	125 kg (276 lb)
LOAD CAPACITY	160 kg (353 lb)
LENGTH	2.3 m (7.5 ft)
WIDTH	1.1 m (3.6 ft)

LUXURY TRAVEL

Touring sidecars are designed to carry a passenger and luggage. The sleek sidecar, the Hannigan GTL (above), is purpose-built for the giant Honda Gold Wing touring bike (see page 8). Inside is a reclining bucket seat with a headrest. Its aerodynamic shape creates a down-force that presses its tyres on to the road for extra grip. A hard top or soft top protects the passenger from the rain.

Passenger

RACING SIDECAR

The fastest sidecars in the world are the Formula 1 racing sidecars that take part in the World Sidecar Championship. These machines have a low motorcycle along one side, with a third wheel to the side. The entire machine is covered with a fairing to make it aerodynamic. Combined with the 1,000-cc superbike engine, this allows speeds up to 290 kilometres/hour (180 miles/hour).

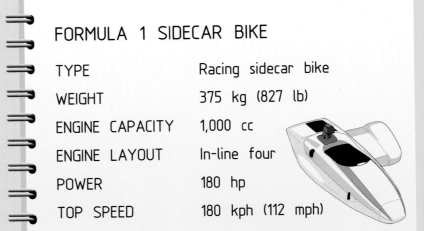

FORMULA 1 SIDECAR BIKE

TYPE	Racing sidecar bike
WEIGHT	375 kg (827 lb)
ENGINE CAPACITY	1,000 cc
ENGINE LAYOUT	In-line four
POWER	180 hp
TOP SPEED	180 kph (112 mph)

A Formula 1 racing sidecar taking a right-hand corner at speed.

SIDECAR DRIVING

A sidecar has a team of two – a rider and a passenger. To stop the sidecar flipping over sideways on corners, the passenger throws his weight over the wheel on the inside of the bend. This keeps the wheel on the ground.

FINDER

www.hannigansidecar.com
Website of the American sidecar maker.
www.superside.com
Website of the World Sidecar Championship.

Driver

TRIKES

A trike is a motorcycle with three wheels instead of two. Most trikes have one front and two rear wheels. Trikes are easier and safer to ride than two-wheelers, and are a popular choice for touring and cruising.

SPORTS TRIKE

The Triketec V2 Roadster is a purpose-built two-seater sports trike. Its long handlebar and low seats give it the look of a giant 'chopper' bike (find out more about chopper bikes on page 16). The 698-cc turbocharged engine and six-speed gearbox gives a fun and exciting ride. It includes high-tech features such as anti-lock brakes.

Engine

Driver's footrest

Passenger seat

TRIKETEC V2 ROADSTER

TYPE	Sports trike
WEIGHT	515 kg (1,135 lb)
ENGINE CAPACITY	689 cc
ENGINE LAYOUT	In-line three
POWER	82 hp
TOP SPEED	170 kph (106 mph)

The Triketec V2 Roadster has its engine at the back, between the two rear wheels.

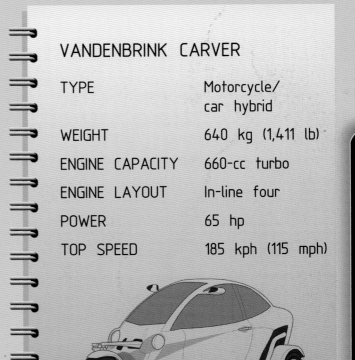

The Vandenbrink Carver has a complex leaning system.

Body leans over

Rear chassis stays level in corner

BIKE OR CAR?

From the inside, the extraordinary Vandenbrink Carver looks like a tiny car. There's a wheel for steering and a lever for changing gear. But when the Carver takes a corner, the body leans over like a cornering motorcycle. The amount it leans is controlled automatically. In sharper turns and at higher speeds, the machine leans more. The maximum lean is 45°.

web

FINDER

www.triketec.com
Site of the Triketec trike company.
www.carver.nl
The Dutch manufacturer of
the Vandenbrink Carver.

VANDENBRINK CARVER

TYPE	Motorcycle/car hybrid
WEIGHT	640 kg (1,411 lb)
ENGINE CAPACITY	660-cc turbo
ENGINE LAYOUT	In-line four
POWER	65 hp
TOP SPEED	185 kph (115 mph)

CHOPPERS

In the 1950s, American motorcycle enthusiasts began to customise their Harley-Davidson bikes. They chopped off any parts that they did not need, in order to reduce weight and improve performance. Typical features of modern 'choppers' are long front forks and a low-slung seat.

CLASSIC STYLE

The Big Dog Chopper is a modern chopper with classic chopper looks. Power from the 1,916-cc engine is sent to the fat rear tyre, which is 25 centimetres (9.8 inches) across. The chopper measures an incredible 2.64 metres (8.66 feet) from end to end.

BIG DOG CHOPPER

TYPE	Chopper
WEIGHT	297 kg (655 lb)
ENGINE CAPACITY	1,916 cc
ENGINE LAYOUT	V-twin
POWER	97 hp
TOP SPEED	Unknown

A chopper bike made by customising a Harley-Davidson motorcycle.

V-TWIN POWER

Like all choppers, the Big Dog machine is powered by a giant V-twin engine. This is the type of engine that all the original Harley-Davidson choppers had. The V-twin is the classic American big-bike engine.

BEAST FROM NEW ORLEANS

The Confederate Hellcat doesn't have the looks of a classic chopper, but is 'chopped' down to the bone. There are no unnecessary ornaments on this bike. Every Hellcat is hand-built from modern materials such as carbon-fibre, aircraft-grade aluminium and high-tensile steel.

CONFEDERATE HELLCAT

TYPE	Chopper
WEIGHT	227 kg (500 lb)
ENGINE CAPACITY	1,850 cc
ENGINE LAYOUT	V-twin
POWER	135 hp
TOP SPEED	240 kph (149 mph)

Triple-beam headlights

Carbon-fibre fuel tank

Engine exhaust pipes

web

FINDER

www.bigdogmotorcycles.com
Big Dog Motorcycles website.
www.confederate.com
Confederate Motorcycles website.

The Confederate Hellcat is built around a lightweight aluminium frame, allowing massive acceleration.

THE FASTEST

The record-holding **EZ-Hook Streamliner** has a tail like an aeroplane to keep it going in a straight line.

You might know about the world land-speed record for cars. There's also a motorcycle, or two-wheeled, world land-speed record, held by the fastest motorcycle on the planet! Many extraordinary and bizarre machines have been built to try to break this record.

RECORD HOLDER

The holder of the motorcycle world land-speed record for wheel-driven motorcycles is called the EZ-Hook streamliner. Wheel-driven means the engine makes the wheels turn, which drives the machine forward. It set the record of 537.6 kilometres/hour (334 miles/hour) in 2003. A streamliner is a bike that is completely covered with a streamlined aerodynamic fairing. This reduces air resistance to a minimum. The EZ-Hook is powered by the engine from a Kawasaki superbike.

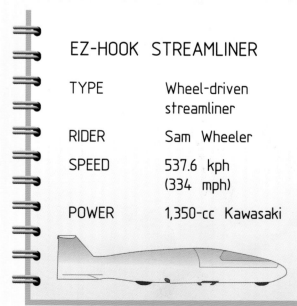

EZ-HOOK STREAMLINER

TYPE	Wheel-driven streamliner
RIDER	Sam Wheeler
SPEED	537.6 kph (334 mph)
POWER	1,350-cc Kawasaki

TRIUMPH STREAMLINER

A streamliner powered by the engine from a Triumph motorcycle broke the motorcycle world speed record in 1956. It reached a top speed of 345 kilometres/hour (214 miles/hour). The engine burned a mixture of methanol and nitrous oxide fuel. The bike set the record at Bonneville Salt Flats in the United States.

STREAMLINER REBORN!

The record-breaking streamliner, nicknamed the Texas Ceegar, was almost destroyed by a disastrous fire in 2003 at the National Motorcycle Museum in England. A team of enthusiasts in Texas accepted the challenge of rebuilding it. The restored streamliner was raced again at Bonneville before being returned for display at the museum.

TRIUMPH STREAMLINER

TYPE	Wheel-driven streamliner
RIDER	Johnny Allen
SPEED	345 kph (214 mph)
POWER	650-cc twin

web FINDER

www.speedtrialsbybub.com
News, information, photos and videos of motorcycle speed trials on the Bonneville Salt Flats.
www.streamliner.com
The E-Z Hook streamliner website.

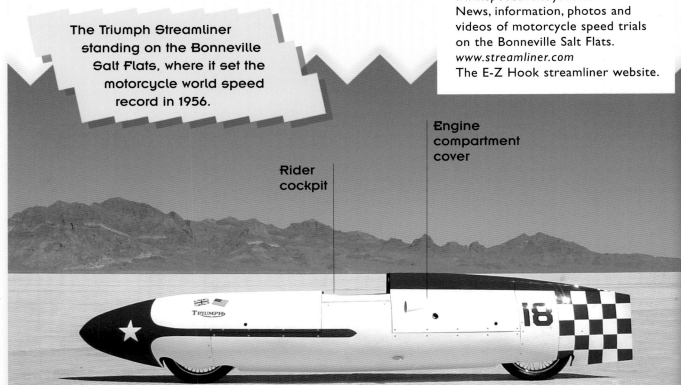

The Triumph Streamliner standing on the Bonneville Salt Flats, where it set the motorcycle world speed record in 1956.

Rider cockpit

Engine compartment cover

TRIUMPH

18

DRAG RACERS

Drag-bike races are short but incredibly fast! The bikes race in pairs along a 400-metre (1,300-foot) straight track. Drag bikes have giant rear tyres that drive them down the track in a cloud of rubbery smoke. They are still accelerating when they reach the finish, and need parachutes to slow down again.

FUNNY BIKE

Funny bikes are one of the types, or classes, of bikes that take part in drag-bike racing. American funny bikes must have a 30-centimetre (12-inch) rear tyre, and wheels that are 2.2 metres (7.2 feet) apart. They consume normal petrol fuel. The rider can also add a chemical called nitrous oxide into the cylinders for an extra boost of power.

A funny-bike drag racer made from a Kawasaki superbike.

Four-cylinder engine

FUNNY BIKE

TYPE	Drag racer
ENGINE CAPACITY	1,248 cc
ENGINE LAYOUT	In-line four
FUEL	Petrol and nitrous oxide
ACCELERATION	0-100 kph (62 mph) in 1 second

Smoke pours from the spinning rear wheel of a nitro-methane-powered top-fuel bike.

Safety bar stops the bike flipping over backwards

Giant rear tyre

TOP FUEL BIKE

Drag bikes in the top-fuel class burn a special fuel called nitromethane. It's the sort of fuel used in rockets! It gives out lots more energy than petrol. Top-fuel engines produce massive power, making the bikes the most powerful and the fastest of all drag bikes. A top-fuel engine gulps down up to 20 litres (4 gallons) of nitromethane in one race.

TOP FUEL BIKE

TYPE	Drag racer
ENGINE CAPACITY	1,400 cc
ENGINE LAYOUT	V-twin
FUEL	Nitromethane
ACCELERATION	0-100 kph (62 mph) in 0.8 seconds

web

FINDER

www.dragbike.com
On-line drag-bike racing magazine.

BIG AND SMALL

There are hundreds of medium-sized motorcycles, some small motorcycles and some big motorcycles, a few tiny motorcycles and a few giant motorcycles! The world's smallest working bike is just 10 centimetres (4 inches) long! And yes, it can be ridden!

THE TALLEST

The world's tallest motorcycle is called Bigtoe. This monster bike is 2.3 metres (7.5 feet) high and 4.7 metres (15.4 feet) long. That's bigger than a racehorse! Bigtoe was completed in 1998 by Swedish bike enthusiast Tom Wiberg, after five years. He included a V-12 engine from a Jaguar sports car, giving a top speed of 100 kilometres/hour (62 miles/hour). The music system consists of four 500-watt speakers.

BIGTOE	
TYPE	World's tallest motorcycle
WEIGHT	1,645 kg (3,627 lb)
ENGINE CAPACITY	6,000 cc
ENGINE LAYOUT	V-12
POWER	300 hp
TOP SPEED	100 kph (62 mph)

Tom Wiberg

V-12, 6,000-cc engine

Structural frame

Hydraulic suspension

The Apache PY80 looks like an adult bike, but is only half as high.

80-cc engine

CHILD'S PLAY

The Apache PY80 is like a shrunken full-size dirt bike. It's designed for children to ride around their gardens and cross-country. Although every part is in miniature, the bike is still exciting to ride. Miniature bikes like the PY50 (right) are called mini motos or pocketbikes. They are not just for children – there are popular mini moto-racing competitions for adults!

Bigtoe is taller, heavier and more powerful than any other motorcycle.

APACHE PY80

TYPE	Children's cross-country
SEAT HEIGHT	650 mm
ENGINE CAPACITY	80 cc
ENGINE LAYOUT	Single
GEARS	3-speed semi-automatic
TOP SPEED	70 kph (43 mph)

web FINDER

biphome.spray.se/bigtoe/
Bigtoe home page.
www.minimoto.com
Mini-motorcycle racing site.

CLASSICS

The best motorcycles of the past are known as classic bikes. The first classic motorcycles were made more than a hundred years ago. Classics might look old now, but they were cutting-edge machines when they were designed. Motorcycle enthusiasts collect these machines and lovingly restore them.

FIGHTING HARLEY

The Harley-Davidson 45 is a classic big American motorcycle that was manufactured by the famous Harley-Davidson company in the 1930s and 1940s. An amazing 88,000 Harley-Davidson bikes were made for the Allied armies in World War II. The rugged machine was used by despatch riders carrying messages. After the war, thousands of ex-servicemen bought the bikes and converted them to street bikes.

HARLEY-DAVIDSON 45

TYPE	Classic tourer
WEIGHT	250 kg (551 lb)
ENGINE CAPACITY	750 cc
ENGINE LAYOUT	V-twin
POWER	25 hp
TOP SPEED	105 kph (65 mph)

This Harley-Davidson 45 is more than fifty years old. It has been carefully restored by its owner.

Fuel tank

Frame

Cylinders of V-twin engine

Exhaust pipes

Twin-cylinder engine

Registration plate

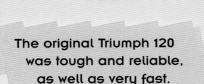

The original Triumph 120 was tough and reliable, as well as very fast.

INTO THE FUTURE

The Triumph Bonneville 120 was built by the British motorcycle company Triumph. The bike was named after the Bonneville Salt Flats in the United States, where a motorcycle powered by a Triumph engine had broken the motorcycle world land-speed record in 1956 *(see page 19)*. The '120' stood for 120 miles/hour (193 kilometres/ hour), the Bonneville's top speed, making it one of the quickest bikes of the time. In 2001, the Bonneville was relaunched with a modern version. This retains the feel and the spirit of the original, with easy-handling chassis and lean, classical styling – but has many modern features as well.

TRIUMPH BONNEVILLE 120

TYPE	Classic superbike
WEIGHT	200 kg (441 lb)
ENGINE CAPACITY	649 cc
ENGINE LAYOUT	Parallel twin
POWER	50 hp
TOP SPEED	190 kph (120 mph)

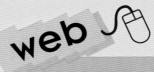

web 🖱️ FINDER

www.harley-davidson.com
Official Harley-Davidson site includes excellent section on the company's classic bikes.
www.triumph.co.uk
For details of the modern Bonneville.

EXTREME MACHINES Motorbikes

CONCEPTS

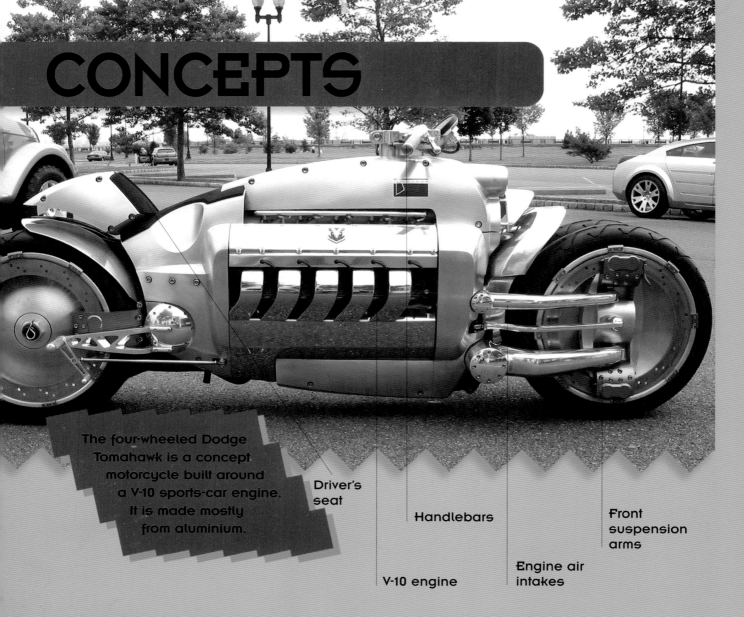

The four-wheeled Dodge Tomahawk is a concept motorcycle built around a V-10 sports-car engine. It is made mostly from aluminium.

Driver's seat

Handlebars

Front suspension arms

Engine air intakes

V-10 engine

What will the motorcycles of the future look like? Concept bikes give us an idea. These are designed by motorcycle manufacturers to show off new technical ideas. Most only ever exist on paper, but some are built for motorcycle shows. A few actually reach the showrooms.

SILVER MACHINE

The extraordinary Dodge Tomahawk concept bike is twice as powerful as a top superbike. Despite weighing as much as a small car, it can reach 100 kilometres/hour (62 miles/hour) in 2.5 seconds! Its V-10 engine comes from a Dodge Viper sports car. There's so much power that the bike needs two wheels at each end, with independent suspension in each.

DODGE TOMAHAWK

TYPE	Concept bike
WEIGHT	680 kg (1,499 lb)
ENGINE CAPACITY	8,277 cc
ENGINE LAYOUT	V-10
POWER	500 hp
TOP SPEED	500 kph (311 mph) plus

HUBLESS MAGNET

The Aprilia Magnet concept bike was designed for the Italian motorcycle manufacturer Aprilia. It's a trike with two-wheel steering at the front and a tilting mechanism for the body. The rider almost lies down to steer. The wheels have no hubs, and are driven by electric motors on their rims. The electricity comes from a generator driven by a 550-cc engine.

web

FINDER

www.aprilia.com/portale/eng/magnet.phtml
Computer models of the Aprilia Magnet.
www.allpar.com/cars/concepts/tomahawk.html
Technical details on the Tomahawk.

Front suspension spring

Electric motors

Driver's controls

V-10 engine

The Aprilia Magnet concept trike's engine drives a generator that provides electricity to electric motors on the wheels.

TIMELINE

1838

A Scottish blacksmith, Kirkpatrick Macmillan, builds one of the first bicycles, with pedals that the rider pushes backwards and forwards to propel it along. The first motorcycles are really just bicycles with engines.

1869

The Michaux-Perreaux motorcycle is the first bicycle powered with a steam engine. The hot engine is just under the driver's seat! Several other steam-powered motorcycles are built at this time.

1876

German engineer Gottlieb Daimler invents the four-stroke internal combustion engine, using petrol as fuel. This is the type of engine used in most modern motorcycles.

1885

British engineer John Starley invents his 'safety' bicycle, featuring a diamond-shaped frame, a chain drive and brakes.

1885

Gottlieb Daimler builds a motorcycle powered by one of his petrol engines, a 264-cc model. It has a wooden frame and small stabilising wheels on each side because it is heavy and unsteady.

1894

The first production motorcycle, the Hildebrand & Wolfmuller, begins to be made in Germany (earlier bikes were one-off machines and were not for sale).

1901

In France, the Werner brothers build a machine with the engine at the bottom of the frame. This is the layout used in all modern motorcycles.

1903

The Harley-Davidson company is formed in the United States by William, Walter and Arthur Davidson, and William Harley. Their first motorcycle is built in 1904.

1903

The motorcycle sidecar is invented.

1905

The chain drive is introduced to motorcycles. Before this, the engine drove the rear wheel with a leather belt.

1907

The first of the famous Isle of Man TT races takes place. The races are still running today.

1907

The world's first proper motorcycle-racing (and car-racing) track, with huge banked corners, was built at Brooklands in England.

1914
The first motorcycle trials race, the Scott Trial, is held in Yorkshire, England.

1920
Speedway racing (racing on an oval-shaped dirt track) is developed in the United States.

1923
BMW launches its first motorcycle, the 500-cc R32.

1929
Harley-Davidson builds the first Harley-Davidson 45.

1935
BMW introduces the telescopic fork on the front suspension of its motorcycles. This is a feature of most modern motorcycles.

1939-45
Motorcycles play an important role in World War II. They are used mainly by despatch riders, but also serve as machine-gun platforms, with the gun in the sidecar.

1948
The Honda motorcycle company is formed in Japan. Honda now makes more motorcycles than any other manufacturer.

1948
The Vincent Black Shadow is the first motorcycle to reach a top speed of 250 kph (155 mph).

1950
American bike enthusiasts begin building the first 'choppers' from Harley-Davidson motorcycles.

1958
The Honda Super Cub, with a 50-cc engine, begins production. It becomes the biggest-selling motorcycle ever.

1959
Triumph begins production of the Bonneville 120.

1968
The Honda CB750 causes a sensation when launched at the Tokyo Motorcycle Show. It is the first motorcycle to be called a 'superbike'.

1968
Italian rider Giacomo Agostini wins the first of five successive Isle of Man TT races on his MV Augusta machine.

1974
American stunt rider Evel Knievel attempts to jump a canyon on a trials motorcycle. He doesn't make it, and parachutes to safety.

1975
The first Honda Gold Wing, with a 1,000-cc engine, is produced.

1988
The first World Superbike championship is held.

1990
The Easy Riders streamliner breaks the motorcycle world speed record.

1992
Honda launches its Fireblade superbike.

2003
EZ-Hook breaks the motorcycle world speed record at Bonneville Salt Flats, U.S.

GLOSSARY

CAPACITY
The volume inside the cylinders of an engine. The bigger the capacity, the more power the engine produces.

CC
Short for 'cubic centimetre', a measure of the capacity of an engine.

CHOPPER
Motorcycle stripped down to its essential parts, with no decoration.

CYLINDER
Space inside an engine in which the fuel is burned to make pistons move in and out.

DAMPER
Device that reduces (or damps down) vibrations.

EXHAUST
System of pipes at the rear of a motorcycle, for carrying waste gases from the engine into the air.

FAIRING
Smooth cover over a motorcycle frame that allows air to flow smoothly over the bike.

FRONT FORKS
Struts that connect a motorcycle's front wheel to its frame.

HORSEPOWER (HP)
A measure of the energy output (or power) of an engine.

IN-LINE ENGINE
Arrangement in which the cylinders are arranged parallel to each other in a line.

L-TWIN ENGINE
Arrangement in which the two cylinders are arranged at right angles to each other.

PARALLEL TWIN ENGINE
Arrangement in which two cylinders are next to each other.

QUAD
Motorcycle with four wheels.

SHAFT DRIVE
Spinning rod that carries power from a motorcycle's engine to its rear.

SHOCK ABSORBER
Part of a suspension system that soaks up the energy if a bike hits a violent bump.

SIDECAR

Small passenger compartment attached to the side of a motorcycle.

SINGLE-ENGINE ARRANGEMENT

An engine with just one cylinder.

SUPERBIKE

Lightweight motorcycle with powerful engine and excellent performance for rack racing and sports riding.

SUSPENSION

System that connects a motorcycle's wheels and frame, allowing the wheels to move up and down over bumps.

THROTTLE

Twisting handle that changes the amount of fuel reaching the engine, and so the power coming from the engine.

TRIKE

Motorcycle with three wheels.

TURBOCHARGER

Device that blows air into an engine's cylinders, allowing it to burn more fuel and produce more power.

V-10 OR V-12 ENGINE

Arrangement in which 10 or 12 cylinders are arranged in two rows at an angle to each other.

V-TWIN ENGINE

Arrangement in which two cylinders are arranged at an angle to each other, making a V-shape.

WHEEL

Cruise control that makes a motorcycle travel at constant speed automatically. Allows the rider to release the throttle.

Note to parents and teachers:
Every effort has been made by the Publishers to ensure that the websites in this book are suitable for children, that they are of the highest educational value, and that they contain no inappropriate or offensive material. However, because of the nature of the Internet, it is impossible to guarantee that the contents of these sites will not be altered. We strongly advise that Internet access is supervised by a responsible adult.

INDEX